PRINCE2®
7th Edition
Practitioner Certification

Question Bank as Mock Exam Paper

Naga Manikanta Kartheek Tavva &
Mahesh Deosthale

Presented by SHARVA GROUP

Qurate
quratebooks.com

Book Creation Services

by

BookMyStory®

It's time you tell your story

www.bookmystorypublishing.com

A venture of

R&S Enterprises

PRINCE2® 7th Edition Practitioner Certification
Question Bank as Mock Exam Paper

Naga Manikanta Kartheek Tavva & Mahesh Deosthale

Published in 2024

© Published by

Qurate
qauratebooks.com

Qurate Books Pvt. Ltd.
Goa 403523, India
www.qauratebooks.com
Tel: 1800-210-6527, Email: info@qauratebooks.com

ISBN: 978-93-58987-26-3

About The Author

KARTHEEK (nagamanikantakartheek@gmail.com)

Kartheek is a certified PRINCE2® Practitioner and Project Lead with over 7 years of experience managing IT projects across global markets. Holding an MSc in Project Management from London, he specializes in Agile, Scrum, Lean, and Waterfall methodologies to drive successful project outcomes.

Kartheek has worked with leading organizations like Wipro Technologies, Tech Mahindra, and Accenture, excelling in project governance, risk management, and process optimization.

He works as a freelance instructor and consultant, for Project Management and helps aspirants to achieve certification and career success.

MAHESH (maheshmd@sharvagroup.com)

Mahesh has 29 years of working for tier 1 organisations in global IT services industries. He specialises into Program and Project Management, Information Security Management, IT Service Management and Software Quality Management.

Mahesh is Approved Trainer from Axels, UK for PRINCE2 v7 and PRINCE2 Agile for Foundation and Practitioner levels. He has successful experience of creating and publishing similar mock question banks for PRINCE2 edition 6 Foundation and Practitioner certification examinations.

SHARVA GROUP, a boutique IT Consulting and Training organisation provides various trainings and IT transformation services across BNFS, Insurance & Manufacturing sectors.

IT Modernization Project

AarMar Shipbuilders, a leading organization in the maritime industry, is undertaking a comprehensive ERP product roll-out to modernise its IT systems. This initiative has been designed to replace legacy systems with a fully integrated, scalable ERP solution that enhances organisational efficiency and supports AarMar's strategic objectives. For this project, AarMar has engaged **SG Tech ERP Systems**, a specialized ERP vendor responsible for the core product implementation. While SG Tech handles the primary ERP setup and deployment, AarMar's in-house IT team will play a crucial role in managing various aspects of the project, including system integration, comprehensive testing, and providing long-term support— comprising roles in Architecture, Development, Quality Assurance (QA), Release Management, and Support—will be actively involved in integration, thorough testing, and ongoing system support, ensuring alignment with AarMar's unique operational needs.

A collaborative approach between SG Tech and AarMar's teams, with distinct phases to oversee progress and ensure quality. This ERP roll-out targets the integration of four critical systems: the Human Resource Management System **(HRMS)**, Customer Relationship Management **(CRM)**, Material Management **(MM)**, and Financial Accounting. By consolidating these essential functions under a single ERP framework, This integration will streamline core processes across AarMar's multi-location operations, facilitating a more interconnected, data-driven environment that supports efficient management and scalable growth. Through this phased approach, overseen by defined roles like the Project

Board and Team Managers, AarMar anticipates a seamless transition that minimizes risks and facilitates efficient change management. With a robust structure for quality control, change management, and continuous monitoring, the ERP roll-out will be a cornerstone in AarMar's journey toward digital modernization and operational excellence.

The high-level project plan is as follows:

Stage 1 (Initiation)

– Assess and design

Stage 2

– Transition CRM and HRMS to ERP

Stage 3

– Transition MM and financial accounting to ERP

Stage 4

– Parallel Run Signoff

Stage 5

– Closure

Additional Information:

Roles:

The Executive — AarMar CEO — is accountable for the project, the key decision-maker, and is responsible for overall business justification. Responsible for approving project scope, and budgets, and making high-level decisions to align the project with business strategy.

Project Assurance — AarMar CFO — plays a critical role in Project Assurance, ensuring that the project remains justified from a financial perspective, and continually assessing its value to the organization. Focuses on providing oversight, quality assurance, and governance throughout the project lifecycle. Ensures financial assessments and benefits realization are tied to the project's deliverables, promoting a focus on tangible outcomes.

Senior Supplier / Project Assurance — SG Tech Client Partner — is to ensure ERP product aligns with project needs, manages supplier resources, and provides insights to the Project Board on supplier-related concerns. Provides guidance and confirms that deliverables align with the agreed specifications.

Team Managers — SG Tech Delivery Manager & SG Tech Product Manager is responsible for successfully delivering and managing the ERP system's development and deployment. Collaborate closely to ensure efficient and timely development processes that align with user needs. While the Delivery Manager focuses on execution and resource management, the Product Manager ensures the product meets business objectives.

Project Manager — AarMar IT Head — took the role of project manager and is accountable for managing from initiation to project closure. Oversees all project activities, manages risks, ensures communication with stakeholders, coordinates resources and ensures compliance with guidelines.

Senior User / Project Assurance — AarMar HR Head — plays a vital role in Project Assurance for the ERP implementation project. This position focuses on ensuring that the project meets end-users' needs, particularly human resource management, and aligns with **AarMar Shipbuilders'** goals. Engages throughout the various stages, ensuring that user needs are considered at every phase of the project.

Senior User / Project Assurance — AarMar Sales Head — focuses on ensuring that the project effectively meets the needs of the sales department and aligns with the overall business objectives of **AarMar Shipbuilders**. Engages throughout various stages, ensuring that the sales department's needs are addressed at every phase of the project.

Senior User / Project Assurance — AarMAr Production Head — ensures that the project remains aligned with the business case by validating that the ERP functionalities enhance production processes and add value to the **AarMar Shipbuilders**. Actively engages in project governance throughout various stages, ensuring that the production department's needs are integrated into every phase of the project.

Project support— AarMar IT Lead— provides administrative and technical support, helps with documentation, testing, and issue tracking, and assists in coordination between AarMar teams and SG Tech.

Questions

Principles

1) **SG Tech ERP Systems** recommended establishing PRINCE2 practices as the first step in implementing the ERP product. Which PRINCE2 principle does this support?

A. **'Focus on products'** ensures quality gates and standardised processes are in place to effectively track and implement the ERP project.

B. **'Manage by Stages'** facilitates handling complex tasks by breaking them into manageable stages, and grouping similar functions for efficient management.

C. **'Tailor to suit the project'** highlights adapting PRINCE2 practices to fit the project's specific size, complexity, and nature, demonstrating customization from the outset.

D. **'Learn from experience'** emphasizes the value of applying a standardized project management method from the start to manage the project's complexity effectively.

2) The project is in the 'starting up a project' process. The **AarMar CEO** has advised that all existing systems should migrate to the new ERP solution with full integration across all locations. This will enable all teams to access existing data through the new solutions. The **AarMar IT Head** has been advised to effectively communicate with all stakeholders across the locations to include everything in this project. Which principle is being applied, and why?

A. **'Focus on products'** because the project manager must identify the necessary products and functionalities to ensure that the new ERP solution meets the needs of all teams.

B. **'Focus on products'** because the project manager should determine the deliverables required for successful integration and data access.

C. **'Manage by exception'** because the project should have clear tolerances for time and cost, allowing stakeholders to focus on strategic decisions while the project team manages the day-to-day operations.

D. **'Manage by exception'** because the project manager should be given the authority to make decisions within the defined tolerances, enabling effective communication and issue resolution.

3) The **AarMar IT Head**, as Project Manager, wants to ensure lessons learned from past ERP implementations are captured and applied to reduce risk and improve outcomes. Which action would best demonstrate adherence to the **'Learn from Experience'** principle?

A. The Project Manager documents lessons from previous system roll-outs and shares them with both AarMar and SG Tech teams, ensuring these insights inform current planning and decision-making.

B. The SG Tech Delivery Manager requires all team members to log issues encountered during each phase, intending to create a comprehensive issue-tracking system for future projects.

C. The AarMar HR Head reviews potential ERP training challenges faced in past projects to tailor training sessions for end-users in the current project.

D. The Project Board mandates that the project's quality control and testing processes follow industry standards, ensuring high standards for each phase of the ERP implementation.

4) During the project, the Project Assurance team, led by the CFO, reviews the project's progress and impact on the organization's strategic goals. They identify that the cost of additional customization requests from multiple departments could exceed the initial budget, potentially reducing the overall ROI. According to PRINCE2's principle of **"Ensure continued business justification,"** what would be the most appropriate course of action?

A. Seek approval from the AarMar CEO to increase the project budget, as these customizations align with specific departmental needs and enhance the ERP system's value across various functions.

B. Recommend limiting customizations to those that align directly with the strategic goals and original business case, ensuring that the project maintains its cost-effectiveness and long-term value.

C. Approve all customization requests temporarily, allowing flexibility in project scope as the departments might benefit from unique features tailored to their workflows.

D. Postpone the ERP project until a new budget can be secured, ensuring the organisation can afford all customizations and avoid overspending mid-project.

5) As The project progresses through its initial stages, the AarMar IT Head, serving as the Project Manager, must clarify the roles and responsibilities of the various stakeholders to ensure effective collaboration between AarMar's in-house IT team and SG Tech ERP Systems. This is crucial for successfully transitioning key systems to the new ERP solution while maintaining alignment with organizational objectives. Which of the following statements best illustrates the principle of **"Define roles, responsibilities, and relationships"** within the context of the AarMar ERP project?

A. The AarMar CEO, as the Executive, delegates all decision-making responsibilities to the SG Tech Delivery Manager, expecting them to manage the project without further input from AarMar's leadership.

B. The AarMar IT Head outlines specific roles for the Project Board, Team Managers, and Project Assurance representatives, ensuring that each stakeholder understands their responsibilities and how they contribute to project success.

C. The SG Tech Client Partner assumes the role of the Project Manager to directly manage the implementation timeline, bypassing the AarMar IT Head's authority to streamline communication.

D. The AarMar CFO decides to limit stakeholder communication to only the Project Board members to minimize confusion, disregarding the importance of engaging all team members involved in the project.

6) The project is divided into stages, with each phase focussing on a certain milestone, such as transitioning CRM and HRMS, then MM and financial accounting. As the project continues to stage 4, a crucial issue arises about data synchronisation between the old and new systems, which could affect operational continuity. How should the **"Manage by Stages"** approach assist the decision-making process in addressing this challenge?

A. **Ensure clear stage boundaries are defined,** so the Project Board can evaluate progress and make informed decisions about whether to proceed to the next stage or extend the current one for additional risk mitigation.

B. **Use regular stage assessments** to review the effectiveness of data synchronization, allowing for adjustments in resources or timelines before the project moves to the final closure stage.

C. **Empower the Project Manager to escalate the issue** to the Executive for a decision, focusing on how best to handle synchronization risks without delaying the transition to the next stage unnecessarily.

D. **Implement contingency plans** developed during earlier stages, ensuring that any unforeseen issues with data synchronization can be addressed without disrupting the overall project timeline.

7) The Project Manager, AarMar's IT Head, has actively overseen day-to-day operations and made various decisions regarding the integration of HRMS and CRM into the ERP system. However, a serious difficulty occurs with the CRM module, where integration is taking longer than anticipated due to unforeseen technological challenges. This delay has the potential to have an impact on the project's timeframe and resources. The Project Manager decides to escalate the problem to the Project Board to explore potential course corrections and resource reallocation. Given that the Project Manager is empowered to address day-to-day concerns, escalation to the Project Board occurs only when the issue exceeds the set cost and time tolerance criteria.

Which **PRINCE2** principle is being applied in this scenario, and why?

A) **'Focus on products',** because the CRM integration issue is directly tied to product quality, and the Project Manager is attempting to match outputs with user expectations.

B) **'Tailor to suit the project',** which means that the Project Manager adapts the ERP solution design to address technological issues without changing the project's scope.

C) **'Manage by exception',** in which the Project Manager escalates the issue to the Project Board only if it exceeds the set cost and time tolerance criteria, allowing the board to make strategic decisions.

D) **'Manage by exception'** means that the Project Manager makes technical choices without engaging the Project Board, ensuring efficiency in day-to-day operations.

People

8) The Project Manager observes a developing conflict between the AarMar IT Lead and the SG Tech Delivery Manager during the project. This conflict results from miscommunications about the allocation of responsibilities, especially about integration and testing, which are essential for the ERP system's seamless implementation. As a result, important deliveries are delayed, and team members are growing impatient with the unclear responsibilities. Following **'leading successful teams'** according to the "people" element, the AarMar IT Head chooses to solve the problem by encouraging improved communication and outlining roles and duties across the teams. What is the most effective way to handle this situation?

A. **Ensure Clear Role Definitions** – The Project Manager should revisit the project's organizational structure and ensure that each team member understands their specific responsibilities. This clarity will prevent overlap and allow team members to focus on their tasks, improving coordination.

B. **Manage by Exception** – The Project Manager should delegate all decision-making to the **SG Tech Delivery Manager** and **AarMar IT Lead**, stepping back to focus only on major escalations. This will allow the teams to operate independently and solve their problems, reducing friction.

C. **Focus on Team Motivation** – The Project Manager should organize team-building exercises and motivational sessions to boost morale. This will help the teams feel better about working together but may not directly address the underlying role conflict.

D. **Re-assign Responsibilities** – The Project Manager should intervene by directly reassigning tasks and responsibilities between the teams to ensure the work is more evenly distributed. This would allow the Project Manager to take control of the project's direction but could reduce team autonomy.

9) The project involves multiple stakeholders, including AarMar's in-house IT team and SG Tech ERP Systems. The project structure is designed with a collaborative approach, where both AarMar and SG Tech teams work together to achieve success. Given the complexity and scale of the project, a critical issue arises during the Transition of CRM and HRMS to ERP (Stage 2). A misalignment occurs in the understanding of user needs between the Sales and

HR departments, causing delays in the implementation phase. This has led to friction between the stakeholders, impacting the overall project timeline. Which of the following actions, based on the PRINCE2 principles related to **'leading successful teams',** should the Project Manager take to address this issue effectively?

A. Prioritize the issue based on urgency and escalate the situation to the Executive for immediate resolution, bypassing team-level discussions.

B. Assign additional resources to the Sales and HR teams to ensure the project moves forward without further delays, leaving the alignment discussion for a later stage.

C. Delay the ERP rollout until the conflict is resolved to avoid further issues and reorganize the implementation schedule.

D. Organize a workshop with the Sales and HR teams and the Project Board to clarify and align user requirements, ensuring that both departments are on the same page and any gaps in understanding are addressed.

10) During the project, the production team raised significant concerns regarding integrating the Materials Management (MM) module. They worry about disruptions to their daily operations and are hesitant about adapting to the new ERP system. The AarMar Production Head, who serves as Senior User/Project Assurance, has noticed a lack of engagement and trust from the production team and has escalated this issue to the Project Manager. To address these concerns, the Project Manager is considering strategies to manage resistance, build confidence, and ensure that the production team actively participates in the ERP transition. Which strategy, based on the PRINCE2 "People" aspect, should the project manager employ to lead this change successfully?

A. Provide additional training sessions to the production team, concentrating on the benefits of the ERP system for manufacturing processes.

B. Create a feedback structure for the production team that ensures their problems are regularly gathered, reviewed, and resolved by the Senior User.

C. Assure the production team that all operational disruptions will be addressed after the system goes live, and concentrate on completing the project on time.
D. Involve key members of the production team in testing the MM module, allowing them to learn about the changes firsthand and contribute to system refinement.

11) The project is in the Transition phase where CRM and HRMS systems are being integrated into the ERP. During this phase, resistance to the new system was observed among several teams, particularly from the HR department, as they felt the new processes might disrupt their established workflows. The AarMar IT Head has reported this resistance to the AarMar CEO and AarMar HR Head. This resistance could affect the project's timeline and the transition's success, making it essential to address it effectively.
A. The **Project Manager** should hold extra meetings and workshops with HR to clarify the ERP system's benefits, address concerns and involve HR in the transition to reduce resistance.
B. The **Executive (CEO)** should mandate the change, emphasizing that the ERP rollout aligns with strategic objectives, to reinforce the project's importance and minimize resistance.
C. The **Senior User (HR Head)** should work with the Project Manager to provide hands-on training for HR staff, helping them adapt workflows and reducing resistance through practical support.
D. The **Project Manager** should adjust the project timeline, allowing more time for HR to acclimate to the new system, easing the transition through gradual adaptation.

12) AarMar Shipbuilders is encountering some issues in the project, and the SG Tech and AarMar teams need to strengthen their coordination. Specifically, there have been delays in aligning testing and deployment efforts with AarMar's specific operating

requirements, and some stakeholders believe the project's communication objectives need to be satisfied adequately. According to PRINCE2's principle of people and relationships, what would be the best approach to address these challenges and ensure successful project outcomes?

A. Enhance Project Board Communication

B. Empower the Project Manager to Facilitate Team Collaboration

C. Involve Team Managers More Directly in Decision-Making

D. Establish Regular Cross-Functional Workshops

13) AarMar Shipbuilders need a structured approach to monitor and assess the impact of integrating the HRMS, CRM, MM, and Financial Accounting systems into the new ERP framework. This includes determining how each system's data and procedures will be incorporated, creating clear quality standards, monitoring the AarMar IT team's engagement, and developing protocols to assure system compatibility and operational continuity across all locations. Under which heading of the change management approach should this information be recorded?

A. Roles and Responsibilities

B. Impact Assessment and Evaluation

C. Change Control Process

D. Stakeholder Communication and Engagement

Business Case

Here are three statements relating to the business case for the project. Under which business case (A-E) heading should the statements be recorded? Choose only ONE heading for each statement. Each heading can be used once, more than once, or not at all.

14) The project is anticipated to face integration challenges due to the complexity of transitioning multiple legacy systems to a single ERP framework, which will impact the timeline. 15) The high-level project plan spans five stages and will take approximately seven months to complete, with stage 2 focusing on CRM and HRMS integration. 16) AarMar considered three options: continuing with legacy systems, partial ERP integration, or a complete ERP roll-out. The chosen option is a comprehensive ERP roll-out for improved operational efficiency.	A. Reasons B. Business options C. Time D. Costs E. Major risks

17) The Project Executive has raised a concern about ensuring that the project remains aligned with the company's strategic goals throughout its duration. Furthermore, the CFO has highlighted the importance of regular financial justification checks to ensure that the project continues to give value for money. As the project moves into Stage 2, unexpected obstacles have arisen, resulting in increased expenses and delays in integrating the CRM and HRMS modules.

Given this scenario, which strategy best reflects the right use of the 'business case' practice, and why?

A. Update the business case at Stage 2 to reflect increased costs and delays, ensuring project viability and alignment with strategic goals.
B. Use the original approved business case from the Initiation Phase for consistency in decision-making despite challenges.

C. Engage the Project Board for an exception assessment of the business case, addressing financial impacts and potential adjustments.

D. Proceed with Stage 2 without updating the business case, managing challenges within expected risks and tolerances.

18) In the 'starting up a project' process, the executive decided it would waste time and effort to produce a business case during Stage 1 of the implementation project. This is because the project team believes that they will not have enough information to determine whether the system is desirable, viable, and achievable until the options analysis is completed in Stage 2. Is this an appropriate application of the 'business case' practice, and why?

A. No, it's inappropriate as the business case should be developed during Stage 1 to ensure benefits, risks, and feasibility are understood from the start.

B. Yes, it's appropriate as detailed system information, necessary for decision-making, can be obtained after completing Stage 2's options analysis.

C. No, skipping the business case in Stage 1 risks starting the project without clear alignment to goals, leading to misalignment and resource waste.

D. Yes, it's appropriate as the business case can be developed after Stage 1, once the project's scope and requirements are clearer following Stage 2.

Organizing

Here are three roles relating to the AarMar Shipbuilders IT Modernization Project. Which individual (A-F) would be most appropriate for each role according to the 'organizing' practice? Choose only ONE individual for each role. Each individual can be used once, more than once, or not at all.

19. Project Manager 20. Project Executive 21. Senior Supplier	A. Chief Executive Officer B. SG Tech Client Partner C. Chief Finance Officer D. SG Tech Delivery Manager E. Head of Sales F. Head of IT

22) Is the appointment of **SG Tech Delivery Manager** and **SG Tech Product Manager** as **Team Managers** an appropriate application of the PRINCE2 'organizing' practice? Why?

A. Yes, because both managers are responsible for managing specific aspects of the ERP project, including delivery and alignment with business objectives.

B. No, because only the Delivery Manager should be responsible for the ERP product delivery, not the Product Manager.

C. Yes, because both Team Managers should report only to the Project Board and not to the Project Manager.

D. No, because the Project Manager should handle both delivery and product alignment roles.

23) Given the context of AarMar Shipbuilders' ERP product roll-out, the AarMar IT Head has been appointed as the Project Manager. The Project Manager is responsible for overseeing the successful implementation of the ERP system, working with SG Tech ERP Systems for deployment, and collaborating with AarMar's in-house IT team. Given the roles and responsibilities, is this appointment an appropriate application of the 'organizing' practice, and why?

A. Yes, the AarMar IT Head's role in defining and managing project aspects aligns with the organizing practice for project execution.

B. Yes, the AarMar IT Head can effectively oversee the project, ensuring coordination between the in-house IT team and SG Tech.

C. No, appointing the IT Head may create conflicts of interest, as they are too involved in day-to-day operations to manage the project objectively.

D. No, the Project Manager should focus on high-level governance, separate from the IT Head's operational responsibilities.

Plans

Here are three actions related to developing the stage 2 plan. Which role (A-F) should be responsible for each action? Choose only ONE role for each action. Each role can be used once, more than once, or not at all.

24. Who should review the stage 2 plan to ensure that adequate time has been set up for receiving input and feedback from the User Group on high-level requirements gathering and options analysis?	A. Business layer
25. Who should prepare the schedule for the requirements gathering work package as input to the stage 2 plan?	B. Project executive
26. Who should provide standards based on previous projects to assist in preparing the stage 2 plan?	C. Senior user
	D. Senior supplier
	E. Project manager
	F. Team manager

27) During Stage 4, the AarMar IT Lead is responsible for testing the ERP system's performance across multiple office locations. The AarMar CEO has underlined that the outcomes of these tests must be consistent with the performance benchmarks established in the start stage. The AarMar IT Head is working with SG Tech on these tasks.

According to PRINCE2's 'plans' practice, where should the AarMar IT Lead look for the specific benchmarks to verify system performance?

A. Quality Management Approach
B. Work Package Description
C. Stage Plan
D. Benefits Management Approach

28) The project has reached the end of its Stage 2. The Project Executive advises that Stage 3 be divided into two parts: Stage 3a, which focuses on moving MM to ERP, and Stage 3b, which focuses on transitioning Financial Accounting to ERP. In addition, to shorten the planning process, the Project Manager has been directed to plan both Stage 3a and Stage 3b before completing Stage 2.

Is the Project Executive's decision an appropriate application of the 'plans' practice, and why?

A. Yes, because planning future stages before the current stage ends helps ensure smooth transitions and avoids delays, maintaining project momentum.
B. Yes, as the 'Manage by Stages' principle advocates breaking complex tasks into manageable parts and planning them sequentially for clarity and control.
C. No, as each stage should be planned only after the preceding stage concludes to incorporate insights from its outcomes.
D. No, because the 'Learn from Experience' principle emphasizes basing plans on lessons from the earlier stage, which isn't feasible before Stage 2 is fully completed.

29) The project is in Stage 1 (Initiation). The AarMar IT Head is reviewing the detailed project activities and ensuring that all system requirements for the ERP roll-out are aligned with AarMar's business strategy. The project team needs to have a clear understanding of the overall ERP product's functionality and design specifications. According to the **'plans'** practice, where should the team managers find this information?

A. Project Product Description
B. Stage Plan

C. Work Package Description
D. Commercial Management Approach

Quality

Here are three items of information relating to the 'quality' practice. Under which heading of the quality management approach (A-E) should they be recorded? Choose only ONE option. Each option can be used once, more than once, or not at all.

30. The ERP system's HRMS module must adhere to AarMar's internal HR policy guidelines regarding employee data privacy and access controls. 31. Before going into production, the SG Tech Product Manager will ensure that the CRM system interacts seamlessly with the financial accounting system and meets all functional criteria. 32. AarMar's IT team will use a testing framework to simulate multi-location usage scenarios for the MM system to ensure data consistency across all offices.	A. Scope B. Supporting tools and techniques C. Resources D. References E. Responsibilities

33) During stage 1, AarMar's IT Lead proposes that a key goal of project quality control should be to ensure that the ERP system interacts seamlessly with AarMar's existing operational workflows and data. The AarMar IT Head disagrees, noting that the primary goal of project quality management should be to ensure that the ERP system meets the agreed-upon specifications and user requirements.

Is this a proper use of the 'quality' practice, and why?

A. `Yes, the solution must integrate the ERP system with current workflows and data to meet the user's quality expectations.

B. Yes, because ensuring that the ERP system adheres to agreed-upon specifications and user needs is critical to meeting the project's quality objectives.

C. No, because providing seamless integration with operational operations and data is a byproduct, not a goal of project quality management.

D. No, because determining whether the ERP system meets specifications is a testing activity, not part of project quality management.

34) During Stage 2 of the project, the Project Manager, AarMar IT Head, identifies that SG Tech requires all AarMar departments involved in this transition to provide complete data sets in a standardised format for the integration to proceed smoothly. The Project Manager documents this requirement in the Quality Management Approach and ensures that data validation procedures are outlined. This document will be baselined before the stage concludes. Is the Project Manager's action an appropriate application of the 'Quality' practice, and why?

A. Yes, because the Quality Management Approach should incorporate all of the quality standards and procedures required for effective data integration.

B. Yes, because the Quality Management Approach should always be baselined before the completion of each project stage to ensure responsibility.

C. No, because this need should be recorded in the Quality Register, which monitors specific quality checks and validations.

D. No, because establishing precise procedures in the Quality Management Approach reduces flexibility during execution.

Risk

The following risk has been recorded in the risk register:_

Here are three items of information. Under which heading of the risk register (A-E) should the information be recorded? Choose only ONE heading for each item of information. Each heading can be used once, more than once, or not at all.

35. The SG Tech Delivery Manager has ensured that CRM integration is completed on schedule. 36. The probability of this risk occurring is rated at 40%. 37. If the risk materializes, it could delay the project beyond the timeline tolerance, impacting the business justification.	A. Proximity B. Impact C. Probability D. Risk action owner E. Risk owner

38) During the transition of the CRM system, users report that the system is not displaying accurate customer data from legacy systems. Should this be entered in the issue register, and why?

A. Yes, because this is a deviation from the planned transition outcome and requires immediate resolution.

B. Yes, because user feedback indicates that the CRM module design needs to be changed, which affects scope.

C. No, because this is a risk that was identified earlier and should remain in the risk register.

D. No, because testing activities should resolve this as part of the transition phase, and it does not need formal recording.

39) During the "Initiation" phase, the project manager has recommended implementing a systematic approach to risk management. Assigning roles for monitoring the risks connected to integrating old systems into the ERP and establishing risk tolerances are part of this. Is this an appropriate application of the 'risk' practice, and why?

A. Yes, because the risk management approach ensures that risks are monitored and controlled proactively, aligning with the project's objectives.
B. Yes, because defining risk tolerances early in the project enables the Project Manager to identify and respond to critical risks effectively.
C. No, because risk management is the responsibility of the Executive, and the Project Manager should not recommend changes to this.
D. No, because risk tolerances are typically defined during the 'Directing a Project' process, not in the 'Initiation' stage.

Issues

Here are three actions. Which role (A - E) should be responsible for each action? Choose only ONE role for each action. Each role can be used once, more than once, or not at all.

40. During Stage 4, a discrepancy in the financial accounting data arises due to a system error. This issue needs immediate resolution to avoid delays in going live. Who is responsible for escalating this issue to the Project Board if required? 41. Who should create detailed work packages for transitioning MM and financial accounting to the ERP during Stage 3? 42. If there is a delay in transitioning CRM and HRMS due to unforeseen system integration issues, who should approve a change request to extend the timeline?	A. Senior user B. Executive C. Project assurance D. Project manager E. Team manager

43) The Project Manager, has identified that the legacy systems' data structure is highly inconsistent across locations, posing challenges to ERP integration. The IT Head records this as an issue in the issue register and immediately informs the Project Board to seek their guidance on resolving it.

Is this an appropriate application of the 'issues' practice, and why?

A. Yes, because issues affecting project scope and deliverables must be escalated to the Project Board.
B. Yes, because the issue register is used to record challenges that impact project delivery and communicate them to stakeholders.
C. No, because the issue should first be assessed, and an issue report should be prepared before escalating it to the Project Board.
D. No, because the Project Manager should have attempted to resolve the issue within the agreed tolerances before escalating it.

44) During Stage 3, the ERP system's integration of the MM and Financial Accounting modules is delayed. The issue is recorded in the issue register, however, the SG Tech Delivery Manager tagged it as 'resolved' without confirming that the delay had been managed or that the integration deadline had been changed. Is this an appropriate application of the 'issues' practice, and why?

A. Yes, because the issue was identified and resolved without any further action required.
B. Yes, because the issue was registered and the SG Tech Delivery Manager resolved it without needing any further input.
C. No, because the issue should only be marked as resolved after verifying that the corrective action has been fully implemented.
D. No, because only the AarMar Project Manager has the authority to close issues related to the project schedule.

Progress

Here are three items of information about the 'progress' of the project. Which management product (A-E) should they be recorded in? Choose only ONE product for each piece of information. Each product can be used once, more than once, or not at all.

45. The project manager receives an update on the options analysis work package's progress, including completed tasks and upcoming milestones. Which management product should this be recorded in? 46. The significant staff turnover at AarMar has caused delays due to additional training for new hires. This should be documented in the ongoing project monitoring. Which management product should be used? 47. Which management product should the progress of Stage 3, including the successful transition and completed testing for Financial Accounting, be recorded in?	A. Exception report B. Daily log C. Highlight report D. Checkpoint report E. End project report

48) The Contracted Project Manager suggests creating a more detailed breakdown of the Stage 2 plan with weekly milestones to track progress. Is this an appropriate application of the 'Progress' practice, and why?

A. Yes, because the project is complex and requires frequent reporting to manage risks across multiple locations.

B. Yes, because this helps control progress and allows quicker responses to issues.

C. No, because the project manager should focus on outcomes and only report major milestones.

D. No, because weekly milestones create unnecessary overhead, and progress should only be reviewed at the end of each stage.

49) The AarMar Shipbuilders ERP roll-out project is in its early Stage 1 (Initiation), with the project team focusing on setting up the project. The Project Manager and IT Head are working on defining tolerances for each stage, monitoring progress, and managing potential scope, resource, and timeline changes. Is defining tolerances and monitoring progress an appropriate application of the 'progress' practice, and why?

A. Yes, because the Project Manager should track progress against the plan and report deviations using defined tolerances to keep the project on track.

B. Yes, because defining tolerances for time, cost, and quality early on ensures the project aligns with business objectives and adapts as needed.

C. No, because the Project Manager should only focus on completing work packages, and overall progress monitoring is the Project Board's responsibility.

D. No, because the Project Manager should wait for stage completions before setting tolerances and monitoring progress.

Processes

50) The project manager has received a change request during Stage 2 impacting the CRM timeline. Which PRINCE2 role should they consult to assess its impact on the business case?

A. Senior User

B. Project Assurance

C. Senior Supplier

D. Project Support

51) The project manager is preparing a plan for high-level requirements gathering and options analysis, which the project board has approved. Which role should be informed about this decision?

A. Senior Supplier
B. Project Executive
C. Project Manager
D. Project Assurance

52) In the context, which includes transitioning the HRMS and CRM modules during Stage 2, is the meeting to finalize requirements for these modules an appropriate application of PRINCE2's **'starting up a project'** process? Why or why not? The project spans multiple phases, with distinct roles and responsibilities for AarMar and SG Tech. Stage 2 focuses on transitioning HRMS and CRM to the ERP system. A meeting is planned during Stage 2 to finalize these modules' requirements.
A. Yes, because stakeholder consultation ensures all requirements are captured for inclusion in the project scope.
B. Yes, because defining the project product description at this stage aligns with PRINCE2's focus on understanding project needs.
C. No, because capturing requirements is a part of the 'managing product delivery' process, not 'starting up a project.'
D. No, because stakeholder meetings should occur after the business case is approved.

53) The project is in the 'initiating a project' process. The Project Manager has finalized the scope, timescales, and aggregated risks for the ERP roll-out project. The updated project brief has been prepared for approval. Which role should approve this updated project brief?
A. The Executive
B. Project Assurance
C. Project Manager
D. Senior Supplier

54) During the 'parallel run signoff' stage, AarMar's production team reports that the ERP system is not fully meeting its operational requirements. The AarMar Production Head suggests modifications.

Which role is responsible for ensuring these requirements are addressed without deviating from the project's scope?

A. Senior User
B. Project Manager
C. Project Assurance
D. Senior Supplier

55) During the 'Directing a Project' process, the Executive approved the transition of CRM and HRMS to the ERP system. The approval was given by a written letter, but no formal meeting with the Project Board was held to evaluate risks or assign resources for this stage.

Is this decision to begin transitioning CRM and HRMS to the ERP system an appropriate application of the 'Authorize a Stage or Exception Plan' activity, and why?

A. Yes, because written authorization from the Executive is sufficient to proceed to the next stage.
B. Yes, because transitioning CRM and HRMS was part of the agreed high-level project plan.
C. No, because a formal Project Board meeting should have been held to review and authorize the Stage Plan.
D. No, because the Senior Supplier must confirm readiness before authorizing the stage transition.

56) In the 'Initiation' phase, the AarMar IT Head decides to appoint SG Tech ERP Systems as the primary supplier responsible for the core ERP implementation. The decision is based on their expertise and experience with ERP product deployments.

Which role is accountable for ensuring the supplier's deliverables are aligned with the project's needs?

A. Senior Supplier
B. Project Manager
C. Project Executive
D. Senior User

57) During the project initiation phase, the decision has been made to assign a key task to a graduate trainee as part of the project team. The Project Manager will mentor the graduate trainee and guide them through the three-stage project. The mentor will oversee the trainee's involvement in key project phases, ensuring they gain practical experience and contribute meaningfully to the project's success. Which role should be accountable for this appointment?

A. Business layer
B. Project Executive
C. Project Assurance
D. Project Support

58) The project is at the initiation phase, and the project manager has outlined the potential risks related to system integration, security, and the impact on current operations. The Project Manager consults with the IT support team, department heads, and a project board to understand these risks and document them in the risk management approach. Is this approach an appropriate application of the 'Risk Management Strategy' activity, and why?

A. Yes, because the Risk Management Strategy should include input from all key stakeholders to ensure a comprehensive view of potential risks.
B. Yes, because the Risk Management Strategy should focus only on technical risks and ignore broader organizational impacts.
C. No, because the risk management approach should be developed later in the project after more technical details are finalized.
D. No, because the risk management strategy should only cover financial risks related to project budgeting.

59) During the 'Controlling a Stage' process, the project manager learns that the integration of the Financial Accounting module is facing delays and will not be completed within the agreed-upon time and cost tolerances. After considering appropriate actions, the project manager decides to raise the time and cost tolerances to

allow the team to finish the work. During which activity should the project manager communicate this change with the Financial Accounting team manager?

A. Authorize a work package
B. Evaluate work package status
C. Capture issues and risks
D. Take corrective action

60) The project is in the 'Controlling a Stage' phase, especially Stage 2. The Project Manager is monitoring the status of the CRM and HRMS work packages and reports back to the Project Board. The Project Manager also determines corrective actions based on prior decisions. Which practice is being used by the Project Manager during this process?

A. Plans
B. Progress
C. Issue
D. Quality

61) During Stage 2 of the ERP roll-out project at AarMar Shipbuilders, the Project Manager receives a checkpoint report from the Team Manager, indicating that the **CRM** and **HRMS** modules have successfully transitioned to the ERP system. However, the (Senior User / Project Assurance) has raised concerns about the product's completeness because the required HR staff training hasn't been finalised yet, despite being a crucial element in the product description. The Project Manager informs the **SG Tech Delivery Manager** that the product is not yet complete and asks to resolve the issue.

Is this request by the project manager an appropriate application of the 'receive completed work package' activity, and why?

A. Yes, because the Project Manager must ensure that all required elements, such as training, are completed before accepting the work package.

B. Yes, because the Project Manager is required to approve the final deliverables and accept completed work packages, including any outstanding tasks related to training.

C. No, because the project manager should immediately proceed to approve the product since it has passed quality reviews and is technically complete.

D. No, because the project manager should document this issue as an 'exception' and escalate it to the Project Board for a decision.

62) The AarMar ERP roll-out project is in the **"Managing Product Delivery" process during Stage 2**, where the CRM and HRMS systems are being transitioned to the new ERP platform. The SG Tech Delivery Manager has completed the CRM module testing and verified that it meets the specifications outlined in the product description. They have informed the Project Manager that the work is complete and have sent a detailed report. As part of the PRINCE2 methodology, the Delivery Manager must also notify another relevant role about the completion of this stage.

Which role should the SG Tech Delivery Manager also notify?

A. Executive

B. Project Support

C. Senior User

D. Senior Supplier

63) The project is in the 'managing product delivery' process in Stage 3, transitioning the Materials Management (MM) and Financial Accounting systems to the ERP. A delay in configuring the Materials Management module has occurred, and the SG Tech Delivery Manager needs additional resources to resolve the bottleneck. They request guidance on whether additional funding can be allocated to hire a consultant to expedite the work. Which role should be consulted about how best to deal with this situation?

A. Executive

B. Project Assurance

C. Project Manager
D. Senior Supplier

64) During the initiation stage, the AarMar IT Head is tasked with gathering input from department heads to define the ERP system's core requirements, particularly for HRMS and CRM. The IT Head conducts stakeholder workshops to ensure all departmental needs are captured and agrees on initial project goals with SG Tech. Which statement explains why this is an appropriate action for the 'starting up a project' process?
   A. Because the Project Manager should ensure the project's objectives are aligned with business needs.
   B. Because the Project Manager should define quality expectations for project deliverables during this stage.
   C. Because the Project Manager should confirm the availability of resources before proceeding.
   D. Because the Project Manager should define the project approach and obtain approval to move forward.

65) During Stage 2, the SG Tech Delivery Manager reports delays in CRM module testing owing to unexpected technical issues. The Project Manager modifies the stage plan to assign additional resources for testing without involving the Project Board. Which principle justifies this action?
   A. Manage by stages, making adjustments as needed to stay on track with the stage plan.
   B. Tailor to the Environment, when the project plan is modified to address particular obstacles.
   C. Manage by exception, as the Project Manager has the authority to address small issues.
   D. Continued Business Justification: Resource allocation ensures project feasibility.

66) In the 'Managing a Stage Boundary' process, the Project Manager has to provide a detailed re-plan of Stage 3 due to a delay in the

MM and financial accounting transition. The Project Manager has reported the situation to the Project Board, and they now need an overview of the remaining work and the risks involved. Which role is responsible for assessing and reporting the risks and ensuring that the replan aligns with the project's objectives?

A. Project Manager

B. Team Manager

C. Project Support

D. Project Assurance

67) At the end of stage 2, the project is in the process of'managing a stage boundary'. The Project Manager, has distributed the end-of-stage report and next-stage plan to the Project Board. An online meeting with the Project Board has been scheduled to address crucial themes for the next phase.

A. Yes, because the Project Manager should ensure that the Project Board is aware that the project is progressing according to plan and continues to be justified.

B. Yes, because the Project Manager should have informal discussions with the Project Board when applying the 'manage by exception' principle.

C. No, because the Project Manager should provide the Project Board with the project initiation documentation to support their decision-making.

D. No, because the Project Board should use the 'directing a project' process to review the end stage report and authorize the next stage.

68) During which step of the 'Closing a Project' process should the Project Manager evaluate the overall project performance and confirm that the ERP solution meets the defined business and user requirements?

A. Prepare planned closure

B. Confirm project acceptance

C. Evaluate the project
D. Request project closure

69) During Stage 5 (Closure), the Project Manager reviews the deliverables and confirms that all project products are delivered in accordance with the agreed-upon requirements, ensuring that the project has reached its objectives before closing. Which practice is being applied by the 'closing a project' process?
A. Business Case
B. Organizing
C. Plans
D. Quality

70) The project is now in Stage 4: Parallel Run Signoff. Following the completion of the crucial module transition, the project manager evaluates the ERP system's integration and deployment across all sites. During the final assessment, the project manager comments that the teams' teamwork, integration processes, and parallel run activities were all successful. The lessons learnt suggest that more proactive stakeholder contact might have improved the transition even further. To improve efficacy, the Project Manager recommends developing a more formal stakeholder communication plan for future projects.
A. 'Prepare planned closure', because the project manager should confirm the project can be closed and close the project log.
B. 'Prepare planned closure', because the project manager should secure and archive project information.
C. 'Evaluate the project', because the project manager should create the lessons report by reviewing the project log.
D. 'Evaluate the project', because the project manager should compare actual progress metrics against the original estimates.

Answers and Rationale Section

Q	A	Rationale
1	C	A. Incorrect 'Focus on products': While PRINCE2 does emphasize quality and standardization, setting up PRINCE2 practices at the outset is primarily about tailoring, not product focus.
		B. Incorrect 'Manage by Stages': Managing by stages refers to structuring projects into distinct phases, which is related to but not the main reason for establishing PRINCE2 upfront.
		C. Correct 'Tailor to suit the project': This principle is applied because PRINCE2 encourages adapting its techniques based on the project's size, complexity, and nature. Establishing PRINCE2 practices from the start demonstrates tailoring the approach to fit the specific needs of this ERP project.
		D. Incorrect 'Learn from experience': Standardized project management from the start is less about learning from experience and more about customizing PRINCE2 to suit the project's
2	A	A. Correct 'Focus on products': This principle emphasizes the importance of clearly identifying and defining the products required for project success. By doing so, the project ensures that the ERP solution is tailored to meet the specific needs of all teams across various locations, ultimately enhancing usability and effectiveness.

		B. Incorrect 'Focus on products': Outlining specific deliverables and outputs essential for the successful implementation of the ERP solution. Clearly defining these deliverables helps align stakeholder expectations and ensures that the project delivers tangible benefits to the organization. However, it should not support the needs of across all locations.
		C. Incorrect 'Manage by exception': This principle allows the Project Manager to concentrate on significant issues that deviate from the planned course of the project. By focusing on critical problems and escalating only substantial deviations, the project can operate more efficiently, reducing unnecessary management overhead and allowing for quicker decision-making. However, this does not explain why the scope of the project needs to be identified.
		D. Incorrect 'Manage by exception': Under this principle, the Project Manager is granted the authority to make decisions regarding detailed work while ensuring that stakeholders are kept informed about key developments. This empowerment fosters agility in project execution, as the Project Manager can address issues promptly without constant approval for minor changes. However, this does not explain why the scope of the project needs to be identified.
3	A	A. Correct: This option best aligns with the 'Learn from Experience' principle because it involves proactively capturing and applying lessons learned from previous implementations, which directly supports reducing risks and improving effectiveness in the current project. B. Incorrect: This focuses on quality assurance, aligning more with the Focus on Products or Manage by Stages principles. C Incorrect: This is aligned with the Continued Business Justification principle, ensuring financial oversight and alignment with organizational goals. D Incorrect: This is aligned with the Continued Business Justification principle, ensuring financial oversight and alignment with organizational goals.

4	B	A. Incorrect: Increasing the budget to cover all customizations, which could affect the ROI and may diverge from the original business justification.
		B. Correct: Aligns with PRINCE2's principle of ensuring continued business justification by focusing only on essential customizations, preserving the project's financial viability and alignment with strategic goals.
		C. Incorrect: Risks compromising the project's business justification by expanding the scope without clear alignment with the initial objectives, potentially increasing costs unnecessarily.
		D. Incorrect: This could unnecessarily delay the project and might not address the critical issue of aligning changes with business justification rather than simply securing additional funds.
5	B	A. Incorrect: While delegation is essential, the Executive (AarMar CEO) must remain involved in decision-making to ensure alignment with organizational objectives. Bypassing input from AarMar's leadership can lead to misalignment and lack of accountability.
		B. Correct: This directly aligns with the PRINCE2 principle of defining roles, responsibilities, and relationships. By clearly outlining the roles of each stakeholder, the Project Manager facilitates effective collaboration and accountability, which are critical for the success of the ERP implementation project.
		C. Incorrect: It violates the principle of defining roles and responsibilities. The SG Tech Client Partner should not assume the Project Manager role, as this would create confusion and conflict regarding authority. Clear delineation of roles is necessary to avoid overlaps and ensure accountability.

		D. Incorrect: Limiting communication to only Project Board members can hinder collaboration and information flow. Engaging all relevant stakeholders is vital for ensuring that everyone understands their roles and can contribute effectively to the project's success.
6	A	A. Correct: The "Manage by Stages" principle emphasises organised control points after each stage. This allows the Project Board to review progress, identify risks, and determine whether to continue or extend the current stage. In the scenario, creating clear stage boundaries enables an informed decision on how to handle the data synchronisation issue, whether by limiting risks within the current stage or revising the plan before progressing.
		B. InCorrect: While regular assessments help to monitor progress, "Manage by Stages" focuses on critical decision points at stage boundaries. Regular assessments alone may not provide the Project Board with a formal opportunity to make key choices about whether to progress or pause the project.
		C. Incorrect: Escalation is an important aspect of controlling exceptions, but "Manage by Stages" entails thoroughly analysing the project at predetermined stage boundaries. Immediate escalation avoids the structured evaluation process inherent in this principle, which ensures a comprehensive review.
		D. Incorrect: Contingency planning is important for risk management, although it does not exactly align with the "Manage by Stages" principle. This idea emphasises systematic evaluation and control after each cycle rather than depending entirely on pre-planned responses to challenges as they arise.
7	C	A. Incorrect: "Focus on products" relates to delivering the defined products according to user expectations, however, the focus here is on escalation due to exceeding tolerances, not product delivery itself.

		B. Incorrect: "Tailor to suit the project" refers to adapting PRINCE2 methods based on project size or complexity, although the scenario is about dealing with project exceptions and escalations, not changing the solution design itself.
		C. Correct: "Manage by exception" is applied here because the Project Manager is empowered to handle day-to-day activities and make decisions as long as they are within the cost, schedule, and quality tolerances. The issue is escalated only if it exceeds certain tolerances, allowing the Project Board to intervene and make the appropriate high-level choices. This strategy ensures that the Project Manager focuses on properly managing the project within specific parameters, while only involving the Project Board for decisions that go beyond those constraints.
		D. Incorrect: "Manage by exception" is not about dealing with technical concerns without addressing the Project Board; it is about making decisions within set limits and escalating as needed.
8	A	A. Correct: In line with PRINCE2's 'Leading Successful Teams' under the 'People' element, the best approach is to ensure that roles and responsibilities are clearly defined. This helps eliminate confusion and conflict, leading to better coordination and collaboration. This approach not only resolves the current tension but also helps maintain efficient project progress and team alignment throughout the lifecycle of the ERP implementation.
		B. InCorrect: It is more relevant to situations where project progress deviates from the plan. Here, it is a communication and role clarity issue, not a major escalation, so it may not resolve the core issue.

		C. Incorrect: While motivational efforts are helpful, they do not directly address the structural or organizational issues related to role conflicts and project deliverables.
		D. Incorrect: This could disrupt team autonomy and may not address the root cause of the issue, which is a lack of clear role definitions. It is better to clarify roles first rather than reassign tasks in a top-down manner.
9	D	A. Incorrect: Escalating the issue directly to the Executive without trying to resolve it at the team level contradicts the PRINCE2 approach of managing by exception and leading teams at the right level.
		B. Incorrect: Assigning more resources without resolving the underlying issue would not address the core problem and could lead to more inefficiencies or misalignment.
		C. Incorrect: Delaying the project is not aligned with PRINCE2 principles of managing by stages and ensuring the project continues progressing with active problem-solving.
		D. Correct: 'Leading Successful Teams' emphasizes collaboration, clear communication, and stakeholder engagement. Because it fosters a collaborative approach to problem-solving, ensuring that all involved parties (Sales, HR, and the Project Board) align their objectives and resolve any misunderstandings. It allows for the issue to be addressed without escalating it prematurely, encouraging teamwork and focusing on the project's long-term success.

10	D	A. Incorrect: While training can improve understanding of the ERP system's benefits, it doesn't fully address the deeper concerns around operational disruptions and lack of trust. Without hands-on involvement in the system's implementation, training may have a limited impact on their confidence and willingness to adopt the new system.
		B. Incorrect: Although a feedback mechanism helps the team feel heard, it may fall short in building trust and engagement if they don't see immediate, tangible results from their input. Simply gathering feedback, even if reviewed by the Senior User, doesn't actively involve the production team in the solution itself.
		C. Incorrect: This one risks increasing resistance, as it asks the production team to wait until the project is complete to see if their concerns are addressed.
		D. Correct: This approach aligns best with the PRINCE2 'People' element by actively involving the production team in the change process. By participating in testing, they gain a hands-on understanding of the ERP system's impact on their workflows and have the opportunity to provide meaningful input, which can improve the system's relevance to their needs. This active engagement fosters trust, reduces resistance, and builds ownership, making it the most effective strategy to support successful change.
11	C	A. Incorrect: Although increased communication is beneficial, holding additional meetings may not be sufficient to address deep-rooted resistance. Direct involvement and skill-building, as in Option C, are more effective for sustainable change.
		B. Incorrect: While a CEO mandate may emphasize the importance of the project, it does not address the underlying resistance or provide practical support for the team's concerns, both of which are essential for effective change management.

		C. Correct: This option aligns with PRINCE2's 'Leading Successful Change' under the 'People' principle by addressing change directly with those affected. The HR Head's involvement in training helps address concerns and empowers the HR team with practical skills, fostering a supportive transition and reducing resistance.
		D. Incorrect: Adjusting the timeline may provide some relief but could also delay project completion without guaranteeing a reduction in resistance.
12	D	A. Incorrect: While better Project Board communication is valuable, it doesn't address the daily operational alignment needed for resolving testing and deployment issues.
		B. Incorrect: This does not add a structured mechanism like cross-functional workshops, which are specifically focused on team-level alignment and issue resolution. The Project Manager's role alone may not bridge the gaps between departments and external vendors without consistent, structured team interactions.
		C. Incorrect: This approach could lead to decision-making at a more technical level, but it doesn't involve all stakeholders in the process.
		D. Correct: Regular workshops promote transparency and help bridge communication gaps, ensuring that stakeholder needs are consistently addressed throughout the project. Fostering collaboration between the AarMar and SG Tech teams, and ensuring the solution meets specific operational requirements through direct involvement of end users.
13	B	A. Incorrect: This would focus on who is responsible for different tasks within the change process, rather than how the integration impacts will be assessed. The scenario requires an approach that tracks and evaluates the impact of each system integration, not just assigns accountability.

		B. Correct: Evaluating how system integrations affect the organization and recording necessary assessments to ensure changes meet project objectives without disrupting operations. Because it focuses on assessing the implications of integrating key systems into the ERP, ensuring alignment with the project's objectives.
		C. Incorrect: The scenario specifically asks for an approach to track and evaluate the impact of the system integrations rather than defining procedural steps for approving or managing individual change requests.
		D. Incorrect: The scenario emphasizes evaluating the impact of integrations rather than focusing on how communication with stakeholders will be handled.
14	E	E. Correct: Integration challenges and their impact on the project timeline due to the complexity of transitioning legacy systems to a single ERP, making it a "Major risk" in the business case.
15	C	C. Correct: Outlines the high-level project plan, including a 7-month timeline and focus on CRM and HRMS integration in stage 2, fitting under the "Time" section.
16	B	B. Correct: Describes three ERP implementation options (legacy systems, partial integration, full roll-out) and the chosen comprehensive ERP roll-out, appropriate for the "Business options" section.
17	A	A. Correct: In PRINCE2, the business case is a dynamic document that must be updated at each stage or if substantial changes occur. Updating it ensures that the project continues on track with the business objectives and gives the most up-to-date data for making educated decisions.
		B. InCorrect: This ignores the need to update the business case as the project evolves, risking outdated decisions that fail to reflect challenges like increased costs or delays.

		C. Incorrect: Unless tolerances are breached, this is not an exception scenario under PRINCE2. Regular reassessment during stage boundaries is more appropriate, avoiding unnecessary escalation.
		D. Incorrect: This violates the principle of continued business justification, risking misalignment with strategic goals and financial viability.
18	A	A. Correct: In PRINCE2, the business case should be developed and approved at the start to ensure project viability, alignment with business objectives, and minimize risks.
		B. InCorrect: The business case must be defined early, even with uncertainties, outlining benefits, costs, risks, and timescales, and should be reviewed throughout the project.
		C. Incorrect: Establishing the business case in Stage 1 is crucial for ensuring efficient resource allocation and alignment with business objectives.
		D. Incorrect: Creating the business case in Stage 1 justifies the project and ensures it aligns with organizational goals, preventing misalignment or inefficient resource use.
19	F	F. Correct: The Project Manager oversees the entire project, managing activities, resources, and communication. The Head of IT is ideal for this role, as they manage critical IT infrastructure for the ERP implementation.
20	A	A. Correct: The CEO holds overall accountability, making key decisions, aligning the project with business strategy, and approving budgets and scope to ensure the project's success.
21	B	B. Correct: The Senior Supplier ensures the ERP product meets project needs. The SG Tech Client Partner supervises the supplier, ensuring the ERP solution aligns with AarMar's objectives and requirements.

22	A	A. Correct: According to PRINCE2, Team Managers are responsible for ensuring that the technical development and delivery of the project are handled effectively. The Delivery Manager focuses on execution, while the Product Manager ensures the product aligns with business goals.
		B. Incorrect: The Delivery Manager and Product Manager both have essential roles. The Product Manager ensures the product meets business objectives, while the Delivery Manager focuses on executing the delivery plan.
		C. Incorrect: While the Team Managers are accountable for delivering the project's outputs, they report to the Project Manager who is responsible for managing the project as a whole.
		D. Incorrect: The Project Manager oversees the entire project, but specific responsibilities like product alignment and delivery management are handled by the respective Team Managers.
23	B	A. Incorrect: While the IT Head's responsibility in defining project aspects aligns with organizing, it should focus more on managing activities rather than setting the overall structure.
		B. Correct: The 'organizing' practice in PRINCE2 ensures clear structure and coordination among stakeholders. As Project Manager, the AarMar IT Head is responsible for managing resources and overseeing the ERP implementation, making their role suitable for organizing and managing tasks with the team and supplier (SG Tech).
		C. Incorrect: Although the IT Head's involvement in daily operations might raise concerns about objectivity, PRINCE2 promotes effective project management through clear responsibility definitions, ensuring coordination between internal teams and the ERP vendor. With proper governance, there is no inherent conflict of interest.

		D. Incorrect: PRINCE2 does not require the Project Manager to be independent of operational tasks but rather capable of managing day-to-day activities. The IT Head's role in overseeing the ERP implementation aligns with this approach.
24	C	C. Correct: Senior Users represent the needs of the end-users and ensure that their requirements are adequately addressed. In this case, checking the plan to confirm that sufficient time is allocated for gathering and analyzing user input falls under their responsibilities.
25	F	F. Correct: Team Managers are responsible for creating detailed schedules for work packages. In this case, preparing the requirements gathering schedule aligns with their role in managing specific tasks and deliverables.
26	D	D. Correct: Senior Suppliers, such as SG Tech, in this case, bring expertise and provide standards or methodologies from past projects to assist in the plan preparation. Their input ensures consistency and alignment with best practices.
27	A	A. Correct: Because it provides details on quality criteria and performance benchmarks defined during project initiation.
		B. InCorrect: It will outline task details, responsibilities, and execution but does not define performance benchmarks or criteria, focusing more on operations than evaluation standards.
		C. Incorrect: It focuses on how the stage will be executed, not the criteria for evaluating system performance.
		D. Incorrect: While it may touch on performance improvements as a benefit, it does not provide the detailed quality criteria or performance benchmarks required for testing the system during this stage.

28	C	A. Incorrect: While planning may seem to maintain momentum, it disregards the adaptive nature of PRINCE2. Without fully understanding the outcomes and challenges of Stage 2, premature planning could result in incorrect assumptions and a poorly informed plan for Stage 3a and 3b, leading to inefficiencies or rework.
		B. Incorrect: While the principle of 'Manage by Stages' supports dividing work into smaller parts for manageability, it also requires that each stage's plan be informed by the preceding stage. Planning Stage 3a and 3b simultaneously before completing Stage 2 undermines this principle by not waiting for insights from Stage 2.
		C. Correct: Because it aligns with the principle of planning at the end of the preceding stage to incorporate lessons learned and ensure the plan is based on the latest available information.
		D. Incorrect: While the principle of "Learn from Experience" is relevant, the primary principle violated here is the PRINCE2 practice of planning at the end of a stage, not "learning from experience.".
29	A	A. Correct: This document defines the scope, functionality, and key characteristics of the product (ERP system) to be delivered. Team managers need to understand the full scope of the ERP product and ensure alignment with business needs, particularly at the initiation stage.
		B. Incorrect: It focuses on the activities within a given stage, detailing tasks and deliverables, but it doesn't provide in-depth information about the product's specifications.
		C. Incorrect: Details specific tasks and outputs related to work packages. While important for task management, it doesn't address the overall ERP product requirements.

		D. Incorrect: Deals with managing project costs and supplier relations, not the detailed design or functionality of the ERP product itself.
30	D	D. Correct: Specifies a compliance requirement (internal HR policy standards) and would be documented under references, as it pertains to existing policies or standards the project must adhere to.
31	E	E. Correct: A specific responsibility in the quality management process. Such details are recorded under responsibilities in the quality management approach.
32	B	B. Correct: The testing framework used to simulate scenarios is a tool in the quality management approach, categorized under supporting techniques to ensure quality.
33	B	A. Incorrect: The quality practice in PRINCE2 focuses on ensuring deliverables meet specified quality criteria, not the operational outcomes.
		B. Correct: PRINCE2's quality practice seeks to ensure that the project's deliverables fulfil the stated quality standards and user needs. Ensuring that the ERP system meets the agreed-upon criteria is an essential component of quality practice.
		C. Incorrect: This is not the correct option. While seamless integration may be considered a project outcome, project quality management is responsible for ensuring that deliverables match quality requirements, such as alignment with workflows and data.
		D. Incorrect: This is inaccurate because PRINCE2 includes testing as part of project quality management. Validating that the ERP system fulfils agreed-upon standards is directly related to quality practice since it ensures compliance with set criteria.

34	A	A. Correct: The Quality Management Approach aligns with PRINCE2 by documenting quality standards and procedures, including data validation requirements, ensuring clarity and adherence throughout the stage.
		B. Incorrect: Although the Quality Management Approach is baselined at the initiation stage, the justification doesn't directly explain why data validation should be captured there.
		C. Incorrect: The Quality Register tracks quality events and outcomes, not standards or procedures, making the Quality Management Approach the appropriate place for data validation requirements.
		D. Incorrect: Defining standards in the Quality Management Approach provides a structured framework for quality activities, while still allowing flexibility during execution.
35	D	D. Correct: This is the individual responsible for implementing actions to reduce or mitigate the risk, assigned here to the SG Tech Delivery Manager.
36	C	C. Correct: Probability reflects the likelihood of the risk occurring, rated here at 40%.
37	B	B. Correct: The impact describes the consequence if the risk materializes, such as project delays and business justification threats.
38	A	A. Correct: This is an ongoing problem that has an impact on project results; it should be noted in the issue register so that its effects and resolution can be monitored.
		B. Incorrect: Although user feedback may result in design modifications, this particular case concerns data accuracy rather than scope adjustments.
		C. Incorrect: Risks are potential future events, whereas this is an actual deviation that needs immediate attention, making it an issue.

		D. Incorrect: Even though testing may fix the problem, it still needs to be officially documented to make sure it is monitored and fixed.
39	A, B	A. Correct: This aligns with PRINCE2's risk practice, emphasizing the importance of monitoring and controlling risks proactively to ensure the project's success. Establishing risk tolerances at the initiation stage is an appropriate step.
		B. Correct: While defining risk tolerances is valid, this explanation focuses narrowly on early identification and response, missing the broader objective of proactive control throughout the lifecycle.
		C. Incorrect: While the Executive plays a key role in overall risk governance, the Project Manager has the authority to recommend risk practices.
		D. Incorrect: Risk tolerances can and should be set during the 'Initiation' stage as part of planning.
40	D	D. Correct: Ensures that critical issues are escalated to the Project Board in line with the 'Manage by Exception' principle.
41	E	E. Correct: Team Managers are responsible for creating work packages to define tasks, deliverables, and resources for specific phases of the project.
42	B	B. Correct: The Executive approves significant changes affecting the project's timeline, budget, or scope.
43	C	A. Incorrect: While issues impacting scope and deliverables may need escalation, recording and immediate escalation without an issue report are not aligned with PRINCE2 practices.
		B. Incorrect: Although the issue register is used to record challenges, escalation without prior assessment or tolerances is premature.
		C. Correct: Preparing an issue report to assess the impact and determine solutions before escalation.

		D. Incorrect: Escalation is not inappropriate, but PRINCE2 requires tolerance levels to guide resolution attempts before informing the Project Board.
44	C	A. Incorrect: The issue is likely still unresolved if the impact of the delay hasn't been verified or corrective actions implemented.
		B. Incorrect: While the issue was registered, the SG Tech Delivery Manager should not mark it as resolved without verifying the impact and corrective actions.
		C. Correct: The issue should only be closed after confirming that corrective actions have been fully implemented and the delay is addressed.
		D. Incorrect: The authority to close issues lies with the person managing the issue, not necessarily the Project Manager.
45	D	D. Correct: This report provides regular updates on specific work packages, tracking their progress. The team manager's update on the options analysis work package will be recorded here.
46	A	A. Correct: This is the correct product, as turnover and extra training have caused delays beyond the planned tolerance, requiring formal escalation to the project board.
47	C	C. Correct: This report is used to give a summary of project progress, including positive developments such as the completion of testing and overall smooth progress in a given stage.
48	A, B	A. Correct: Valid, as the project's complexity and multiple locations justify frequent progress checks to manage risks.
		B. Correct: Regular updates help identify and address emerging issues early in a complex project.

		C. Incorrect: While focusing on outcomes is important, the 'Progress' practice in PRINCE2 emphasizes regular monitoring to ensure that progress is on track and risks are managed throughout the project, not just at major milestones.
		D. Incorrect: This is incorrect because frequent monitoring, particularly in complex projects, is essential for managing progress, ensuring that risks are mitigated, and the project stays aligned with objectives.
49	B	A. Incorrect: It focuses on ongoing progress monitoring, while the question is about setting tolerances at the beginning of the project.
		B. Correct: Because it highlights the importance of defining tolerances during Stage 1 to align the project with business objectives and address changes proactively.
		C. Incorrect: The Project Manager is responsible for monitoring progress and managing work packages, not just the Project Board.
		D. Incorrect: PRINCE2 advises setting tolerances early, not waiting until stage completion.
50	B	A. Incorrect: Although they assess functional impacts, they don't focus on the project's business case or overall justification.
		B. Correct: Ensures the project stays aligned with its business case and evaluates changes' impact on justification, timeline, and costs.
		C. Incorrect: They are responsible for the technical aspects, not the financial or strategic impact on the business case.
		D. Incorrect: Their role is more operational, assisting with project management tasks, not assessing the project's alignment with business goals or financial justification.

51	B	A. Incorrect: This role focuses on ensuring the product meets requirements but does not need to be informed about the approval of the high-level plan.
		B. Correct: The Project Executive is accountable for the overall success of the project and should be informed of major decisions, including the approval of the high-level plan.
		C. Incorrect: The Project Manager prepares and manages the plan but does not need to be informed about its approval since they are directly involved in creating it.
		D. Incorrect: This role monitors project alignment with business objectives and financial oversight but does not need to be directly informed of the approval decision, as the Project Executive holds overall responsibility for major decisions.
52	A	A. Correct: The 'starting up a project' process in PRINCE2 emphasizes understanding the project's high-level requirements and ensuring stakeholder needs are considered to define the project scope accurately.
		B. Incorrect: Defining the project product description is not primarily done during 'starting up a project.' Instead, it is a focus of the 'initiating a project' phase, which involves detailed planning based on initial requirements and the approved business case.
		C. Incorrect: Capturing requirements at a high level is indeed part of 'starting up a project,' where initial scoping and stakeholder engagement occur. 'Managing product delivery' focuses on executing detailed requirements already defined earlier, such as coding or configuring the CRM and HRMS.

		D. Incorrect: Stakeholder meetings are essential during the early stages of the project to inform the business case and ensure alignment. Waiting until after business case approval would delay the project and could lead to scope misalignment or overlooked stakeholder requirements.
53	A	A. Correct: The Executive is accountable for the project's overall business justification and must approve the project brief to ensure alignment with organizational objectives.
		B. Incorrect: This role provides oversight and assurance, but it does not have the authority to approve the project brief.
		C. Incorrect: The Project Manager prepares and submits the project brief but does not approve it.
		D. Incorrect: The Senior Supplier focuses on supplier-related concerns and does not have the responsibility for approving the project brief.
54	A	A. Correct: The Senior User ensures that the ERP system meets user needs and proposes necessary adjustments within the project's scope.
		B. Incorrect: The Project Manager facilitates changes but relies on user input to identify requirements.
		C. Incorrect: This role monitors the process but does not directly ensure user needs are met.
		D. Incorrect: The Senior Supplier ensures deliverables meet technical specifications but does not focus on operational requirements.
55	C	A. Incorrect: PRINCE2 requires a formal review and documented approval from the Project Board, not just the Executive's authorization, to ensure alignment and accountability.
		B. Incorrect: While transitioning CRM and HRMS was planned, the Stage Plan must be authorized through the formal 'Authorize a Stage or Exception Plan' activity.

		C. Correct: PRINCE2 mandates that the Project Board reviews and authorizes each stage to ensure readiness and resource availability.
		D. Incorrect: While the Senior Supplier assures deliverables, the formal authorization process lies with the Project Board, not solely the Senior Supplier.
56	A	A. Correct: The Senior Supplier ensures that the supplier's deliverables meet the project's requirements and align with the overall goals. This role is responsible for managing supplier resources and ensuring quality.
		B. Incorrect: While the Project Manager manages the project, they do not directly oversee supplier deliverables from a quality assurance perspective.
		C. Incorrect: The Project Executive is accountable for the project as a whole but is not responsible for supplier deliverables.
		D. Incorrect: The Senior User represents the users but does not oversee supplier performance.
57	D	A. Incorrect: This role ensures strategic alignment but is not involved in the direct management or appointment of project team members.
		B. Incorrect: While the Project Executive is ultimately accountable for the project's success, they typically don't handle team member appointments at the operational level.
		C. Incorrect: This role is focused on oversight and quality assurance, not directly responsible for individual appointments within the project.
		D. Correct: As the Project Support role helps with project coordination, including supporting and mentoring team members, they are accountable for overseeing and guiding the graduate trainee's involvement in the project.

58	A	A. Correct: This is an appropriate approach because the risk management strategy must involve input from all stakeholders, including key department heads and project support, to identify and assess risks from all perspectives.
		B. Incorrect: This is incorrect because the risk management strategy should cover both technical and organizational risks to ensure the project is comprehensively assessed for potential issues across all dimensions.
		C. Incorrect: This is incorrect because the risk management strategy is developed early in the project during the initiation phase to ensure risks are identified and addressed proactively from the beginning of the project.
		D. Incorrect: This is incorrect because the risk management strategy should cover all types of risks - technical, operational, security, and financial—not just financial risks related to budgeting.
59	B	A. Incorrect: This activity focuses on approving the detailed work and setting expectations for what needs to be done, but it is not the point of modifying tolerances during the project.
		B. Correct: The project manager assesses the work package's status and determines if there are any variances. It's here that the decision to increase time and cost tolerances would typically be made in response to the delays.
		C. Incorrect: This step involves identifying and recording any issues or risks that might impact the project but doesn't directly involve negotiating changes in project tolerances, which is a more active decision-making process.

		D. Incorrect: Taking corrective action involves addressing deviations from the project plan, but adjusting time and cost tolerances is more a part of evaluating work package status than taking corrective actions.
60	B	A. Incorrect: This practice involves setting up, maintaining, and updating project plans. It is not directly related to reviewing the current stage progress or corrective actions taken for work packages, so this is not the correct option.
		B. Correct: This practice focuses on monitoring the actual progress of the project against the plan and taking corrective actions if necessary. The Project Manager's review of progress and corrective actions indicates that the Progress practice is being applied here.
		C. Incorrect: The Issue practice deals with identifying, escalating, and managing issues that arise. Since the focus is on monitoring progress and not necessarily dealing with a new or escalated issue, this is not the correct choice.
		D. Incorrect: This practice involves ensuring that the project's outputs meet the specified quality standards. While important, it is not directly related to tracking progress and corrective actions for the work packages, so this is not the correct option.
61	A	A. Correct: The Project Manager is responsible for confirming that all components of the work package, including essential deliverables like training, are complete before formally accepting it. This ensures that the product is fully ready for the next stage.
		B. Incorrect: While the Project Manager approves work packages, they cannot accept the package if it is incomplete (i.e., training is missing). The acceptance requires that all elements specified in the product description are delivered.

		C. Incorrect: Quality reviews confirm that the product meets specified standards but do not account for the completeness of all necessary activities (e.g., training). Approval can only happen once all deliverables are complete.
		D. Incorrect: This situation is a matter of ensuring the completion of a work package rather than an exceptional situation requiring escalation. The issue should be addressed at the team level, not escalated unless it impacts the overall project significantly.
62	C	A. Incorrect: Accountable for business justification and high-level decisions but not routine updates like module testing unless it impacts the business case.
		B. Incorrect: Provides administrative support and documentation but is not the primary role for work completion updates.
		C. Correct: Represents end-users and ensures deliverables meet their needs. Notifying them (e.g., AarMar HR Head for HRMS) aligns with operational requirements.
		D. Incorrect: Oversees supplier deliverables, but notifying them is redundant as the SG Tech Delivery Manager represents the supplier.
63	C	A. Incorrect: Responsible for overall project direction but only intervenes in significant deviations requiring scope or budget changes.
		B. Incorrect: Ensures financial viability and project justification but does not handle operational decisions like resource allocation.
		C. Correct: Manages project activities, including resource allocation and risk handling. Would assess delays and consult the Project Board if approvals are needed.
		D. Incorrect: Ensures deliverables meet specifications and advises on resource needs but cannot make funding decisions.

64	D	A. Incorrect: ligning project objectives with business needs is essential, but this task is part of the ongoing business justification, not specifically 'starting up a project.'
		B. Incorrect: uality expectations are defined later during 'initiating a project.'
		C. Incorrect: While resource availability is considered during planning, this isn't the focus of this process.
		D. Correct: In 'starting up a project,' defining the project approach and securing approval to proceed are key actions.
65	C	A. Incorrect: While stage management is relevant, this situation highlights delegated authority.
		B. Incorrect: Tailoring focuses on adapting PRINCE2 methods, not operational adjustments.
		C. Correct: The Project Manager's ability to address minor issues without escalation aligns with 'Manage by Exception.'
		D. Incorrect: This principle ensures project viability, but it does not directly apply to this action.
66	A	A. Correct: The Project Manager is responsible for the overall planning and risk management of the project. They are required to provide a detailed re-plan, identify risks, and ensure that the project stays on track..
		B. Incorrect: While the Team Manager oversees the technical development of the ERP system, they do not handle the overall risk assessment and reporting at the stage boundary level.
		C. Incorrect: Project Support provides technical and administrative support, such as documentation and issue tracking, but does not lead the risk management or re-planning process.

		D. Incorrect: Project Assurance ensures the project aligns with its goals and objectives but does not handle detailed risk assessments or re-planning during the stage boundary process.
67	A	A. Correct: Reflects the PRINCE2 principle of maintaining business justification, which ensures that the project's ongoing value and progress align with the original plan.
		B. Incorrect: This is incorrect because "manage by exception" is about delegating decisions to the Project Manager and only escalating issues when deviations occur. Informal discussions are not directly linked to this principle.
		C. Incorrect: This is incorrect because the Project Board already has sufficient information at the end of each stage in the form of the end stage report and next stage plan, not necessarily the project initiation documentation.
		D. Incorrect: This option is partially correct, but the Project Board does review and authorize the next stage, making this activity appropriate under PRINCE2's process of managing stage boundaries.
68	C	A. Incorrect: This is the preparation phase where project completion is planned, but it does not involve evaluating the project performance.
		B. Incorrect: This step involves ensuring that the product meets the acceptance criteria and is formally accepted by stakeholders, but it doesn't assess the entire project performance.
		C. Correct: In this step, the overall performance of the project is reviewed to assess whether it met the business and user requirements.
		D. Incorrect: This is the formal request to close the project but does not involve evaluating performance.

69	A	A. Correct: The Business case is key during the 'closing a project' process. The project manager ensures the project has delivered the defined benefits and aligns with organizational goals before closure.
		B. Incorrect: Organizing focuses on project structure and roles at the start, not at closure, which is about validating objectives and deliverables.
		C. Incorrect: Plans are important throughout, but the closing process focuses on confirming that all products have been delivered and the project's outcomes met.
		D. Incorrect: Quality is ongoing, but during closure, the focus is on confirming that products meet standards and the project has achieved its goals.
70	C	A. Incorrect: This activity confirms project completion and ensures all administrative tasks are done, but it's not primarily for recording lessons or recommendations.
		B. Incorrect: This phase secures and archives project information but focuses on documentation rather than evaluating the project or recording lessons.
		C. Correct: This is the correct activity, where the project manager reviews the project and records lessons learned, including recommendations for improving stakeholder communication.
		D. Incorrect: This phase focuses on comparing actual outcomes to estimates, not on generating lessons learned or recommendations, so it's not directly related to improving stakeholder communication.

Email ID:

Mahesh - (maheshmd@sharvagroup.com)

Kartheek - (nagamanikantakartheek@gmail.com)